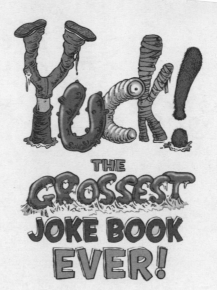

YUCK!

THE GROSSEST JOKE BOOK EVER!

KINGFISHER
a Houghton Mifflin Company imprint
222 Berkeley Street
Boston, Massachusetts 02116
www.houghtonmifflinbooks.com

First published in 2004
2 4 6 8 10 9 7 5 3 1

LIBRARY OF CONGRESS CATALOGING–IN–PUBLICATION DATA
has been applied for.

ISBN 0-7534-5709-1

Printed in India
1TR/0104/AJT/FR(PICA)/90WFO

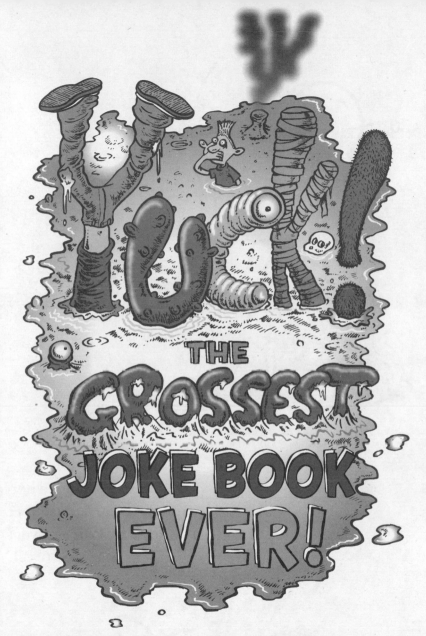

YUK! THE GROSSEST JOKE BOOK EVER!

Illustrated by **Martin Chatterton**

KINGFISHER
BOSTON

Did you hear the one about the constipated mathematician?
He worked it out with a pencil.

What do you get when you run over a parakeet with a lawn mower?
Shredded tweet.

4

Man: I'd like some toilet paper, please.
Lady: What color would you like?
Man: Just give me white, I'll color it myself!

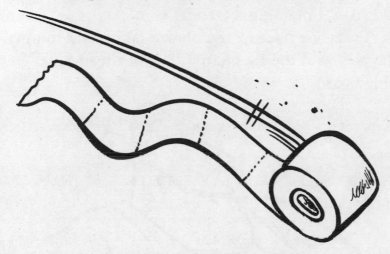

How many farts does it take
to make a stink bomb?
A phew.

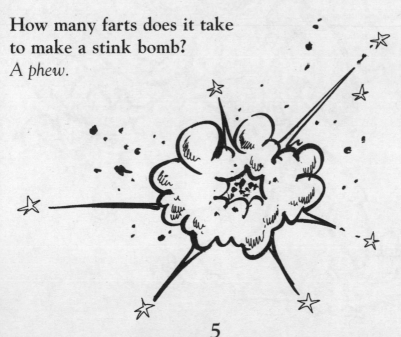

Little Johnny is approached by the lifeguard at the public swimming pool.
"You're not allowed to pee in the pool," said the lifeguard. "I'm going to report you."
"But everyone pees in the pool," said Little Johnny.
"Maybe," said the lifeguard, "but not from the diving board!"

If H_2O is on the inside of a fire hydrant, what is on the outside?

K9P.

Birdie, birdie in the sky,
Dropped some white stuff in my eye,
I'm a big girl, I won't cry,
I'm just glad that cows don't fly.

Taylor: My friend is built upside down . . .

Stacey: *What do you mean?*

Taylor: His nose runs,
and his feet smell!

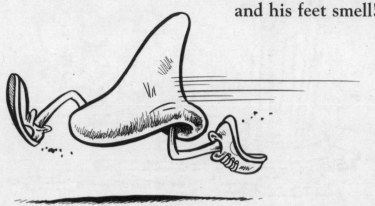

Why did the toilet paper
roll down the hill?
*Because it wanted to
get to the bottom!*

**What do you call a man
with no legs?**
Neil.

What is black-and-white and red all over?
A nun in a blender.

What's invisible and smells like bananas?
Monkey farts.

What's the last thing to go through a fly's mind before he hits the windshield?
His butt.

What did Data see in the toilet?
The Captain's Log.

What is Beethoven doing in his grave?
Decomposing.

Why did Tigger look in the toilet?
He was searching for Pooh.

A belch is just one gust of wind
That cometh from the heart,
But should it take the
Downward route
It turns into a fart.

What's green and smelly?
The Incredible Hulk's farts.

**What's the sharpest thing
in the world?**
*A fart. It goes through your pants
and doesn't even leave a hole.*

**"Mom, mom, I don't want
to visit grandma today."**
"Shut up and keep digging."

Three very thirsty men were stranded in the desert and came across a magician. The magician was standing at the top of a slide. The magician said, "You may each go down the slide, asking for a drink. When you reach the bottom, you will land in a huge refreshing pool of the drink you have asked for."

The first man went down and yelled, "Lemonaaaaaaaade!"

The second man went down and yelled, "Cooooooooke!"

The third man went down and yelled, "Wheeeeeeeeee!"

What did the first cannibal say to the second cannibal after they had eaten a clown?
"Is it me or did that taste a little bit funny?"

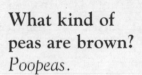

What kind of peas are brown?
Poopeas.

Why did the boy bring toilet paper to the birthday party?
Because he's a party pooper.

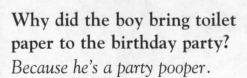

15

A priest was asked over for dinner by one
of his parishioners who had a reputation for
being a little messy.
When he sat down at the table, the priest noticed
that the dishes were the dirtiest that he had ever
seen in his life. "Were these dishes ever washed?"
he asked his hostess, running his fingers over
the grime.
She replied, "They're as clean as soap and water
could get them."
The priest felt a little apprehensive but blessed the
food anyway and started eating. It was really
delicious, despite the dirty dishes, and he said so.
When dinner was over, the hostess took the dirty
dishes outside and yelled to her dogs, "Here, Soap!
Here, Water!"

What's big and gray and has body odor problems?
A smellyphant.

**What did the kid say
to the school cook?**
*"Excuse me, are these
sesame seeds, or have
you just sneezed?"*

What's yellow, brown, and hairy?
*Grilled cheese dropped
on the carpet.*

First man: My dog's got no nose.
Second man: How does he smell?
First man: Awful.

I sat next to a duchess at tea,
It was just as I feared it would be.
Her rumbling abdominal
Was simply phenomenal,
And everyone thought it was me.

What's green and
white and swings
through trees?
Tarzan's hankie!

A little boy asked his teacher if he could go to the bathroom.
"Only if you can recite the alphabet," said the teacher.
"Okay," said the boy. "ABCDEFGHIJ KLMNOQRSTUVWXYZ."
"Where's the P?" asked the teacher.
"Halfway down my leg," said the boy.

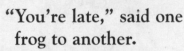

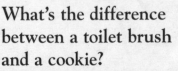

"You're late," said one frog to another.
"I know," he replied.
"I got stuck in somebody's throat."

What's the difference between a toilet brush and a cookie?
You can't dip a toilet brush in your hot chocolate.

"Doctor, doctor, I think I've been
   bitten by a vampire."
"Here, drink this glass of water."
"Will that make me feel better?"
*"No, but we'll be able to see if your
   neck leaks!"*

A boy walks into a store
with a big pile of dog poo
in his hand.
He looks at the store
assistant and says, "Phew,
look at that. And to think,
I almost stepped in it!"

As Terry was getting ready
to go to school, a button
fell off of his shirt. When
he opened his bedroom
door, the handle fell off.
*Now he's afraid to blow
his nose!*

20

Did you hear the joke about the fart?
You don't want to, it stinks!

What do you call a fairy that hasn't washed?
Stinkerbell.

"Waiter, waiter, can you explain why there are footprints in my food?"
"Well, you rushed in, asked for a large omelette, and told me to step on it!"

Mary had a little lamb,
Peter had a pup,
Chrissy had a crocodile
That ate the others up.

What's the difference
between a brussels sprout
and a booger?
*You can't get a kid to eat
a brussels sprout.*

22

What does the Queen do if she breaks wind?
She issues a royal pardon.

What smells, runs all day, and lies around at night with its tongue hanging out?
A pair of old tennis shoes.

**What do you call
a dirty Teletubby?**
Stinky-winky.

Son: Mommy, can I lick the bowl?
Mom: No! Flush like everyone else.

What's brown and sounds like a bell?
Dung.

There was an old man from Oket,
Who went for a ride in a rocket.
The rocket went bang,
His ears went twang,
And he found his nose in his pocket!

Melissa: Do you know anyone who has been on the TV?
Jason: My little brother did once, but he uses the toilet now.

What do you get if you put a young goat in a blender?
A crazy, mixed-up kid!

What vegetable can
you find in the toilet?
A leak!

Jane: My uncle died last Sunday. He had
a heart attack when he was in the
garden picking beans.
Bill: How terrible! What did your poor
aunt do?
Jane: Oh, she had to use frozen beans
instead.

An elderly woman is riding in an elevator in a very luxurious hotel when a young, beautiful woman gets in, smelling of expensive perfume. She turns to the old woman and says, snootily, "It's called *Romance*, and it cost $50 a bottle."

Then another young and beautiful woman smelling of perfume gets in and says, also very snootily, "*Eternal*, $100 a bottle."

Around three floors later the elderly woman has reached her destination and is about to leave the elevator. She turns around, looks right into the eyes of both young women, farts loudly, and says, "Broccoli—49 cents a pound!"

"Mommy, why can't we have
a garbage can like other people?"
"Shut up and keep eating!"

"Doctor, doctor, do the tests show that I'm normal?"
"Yes, yes, both your heads are fine."

A woman with a dog was waiting at a bus stop when a man walked by eating a hamburger. The dog's nose twitched, and he looked at the man's food.

"He likes the smell," the man said to the lady. "Do you mind if I throw him a little bit?"

"Not at all," she replied.

So the man picked up the dog and threw him across the road..

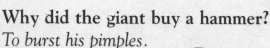

Why did the giant buy a hammer?
To burst his pimples.

Mom: Why don't you go and play soccer
with your little brother?
Brandon: I'm bored of kicking him around.

Darren came home from school with blood on his
face and a black eye.
"Who did this to you?" asked his mother.
"I don't know," said Darren, "but I'd recognize
him if I met him again. I've got one of his ears
in my pocket!"

Where's the best place to have the school nurse's office?
Next to the cafeteria.

What do you get if you cross a skunk with a dinosaur?
A stinkasaurus.

What did the absentminded skunk say when the wind changed direction?
"Ah, it's all coming back to me now!"

Teacher: Your son is very full of himself, isn't he?
Mother: Well, only when he's been biting his nails and picking his nose.

Knock, knock!
Who's there?
Sonia.
Sonia who?
Sonia shoe,
wipe it off before
you come in.

Has the bottom fallen out
of your world?
Eat prunes, then the world will
fall out of your bottom.

What did the biker have written
on the back of his leather jacket?
If you can read this, my girlfriend
has fallen off!

Man: How much are those kittens in the window?
Pet Store Owner: Ten dollars apiece.
Man: How much is a whole one?

What's the difference between school lunches and horse poo?
School lunches are usually cold.

Why did the hedgehog cross the road?
To show that he had guts.

Knock, knock!
Who's there?
Ivan.
Ivan who?
Ivan itchy bottom.

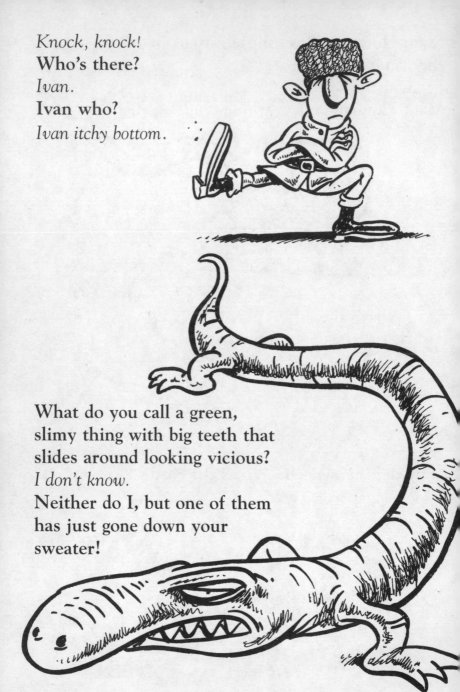

What do you call a green, slimy thing with big teeth that slides around looking vicious?
I don't know.
Neither do I, but one of them has just gone down your sweater!

Dachshund dog
Crossing street,
Speeding car,
Sausage meat!

What's wet, brown,
and smells like peanuts?
Elephant puke.

What happened to the boy
who drank eight cans of cola?
He brought 7 UP™.

Tom had to go to the doctor because every time he tried to speak he farted.

"You must (*ffffaaaart*) help me, Doctor, it's so (*whwhhifflleeee*) embarrassing. The only good thing (*pffllllpffllll*) is that my farts (*sssphhhhwhee*) don't smell."

"Hmmm," said the doctor. "I will have to send you to a specialist."

"Will that be (*ffffaaaart*) a bottom specialist or a (*pffllllpffllll*) surgeon?" asked Tom.

"Neither," said the doctor. "I'm sending you to a nose specialist. There's something very wrong with yours!"

What do you call a green fly with no eyes, no legs, and no wings?
A booger.

How long is a minute?
Depends how desperately you have to go.

Mom: Don't you know that reaching over the table for cupcakes is bad manners? You can always ask me to pass them. Haven't you got a tongue?
Max: Yes, but my arms are longer.

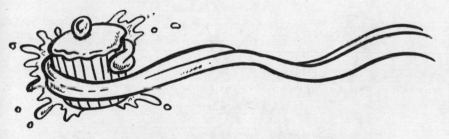

Lisa: My rich uncle fell off of a cliff last week.
Alice: Were you very close?
Lisa: Just close enough to push.

Why did the cannibal join the police force?
So he could grill his suspects.

Did you hear about the stupid dog that laid down to eat a bone?
When he stood up, he only had three legs.

Why can't you hear a pterodactyl go to the bathroom?
Because it has a silent "p."

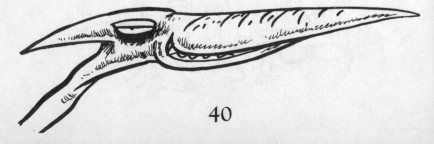

Pete: Mom! Everyone at school says I look like a werewolf!
Mom: Oh, just be quiet and comb your face.

What did the lion say as a busload of tourists came to the safari park?
"Yummy! Here comes meals-on-wheels!"

Mrs. Judd: I need to lose twenty pounds.
Mrs. Sutton: Well, why not chop your head off, then!

Who exploded at Waterloo?
Napoleon Blownapart.

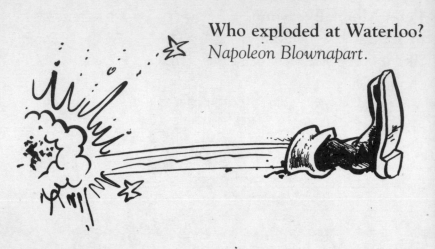

"Waiter, waiter, what's on the menu?"
"Well, I have fried liver, steamed tongue, and frogs' legs."
"Don't tell me your problems, just get me the menu!"

Lawyer in court: And did you see the defendant bite off Mrs. Jenning's nose?
Witness: No, but I saw him spit it out afterward!

Notice in café: *All the drinking water in this café has been passed by the manager.*
Notice in bathroom: *In the interest of economy please use both sides of the toilet paper.*
Notice in butcher's: *Will customers please refrain from sitting on the bacon slicer as we are getting a little behind with our orders!*

What goes ho ho, plop plop?
Santa Claus on the toilet.

43

"Doctor, doctor, I've got so much wind.
Do you have anything for it?"
"Yes, here's a kite. Now go and fly it!"

"Mom, Mom, come quick,
Dad just fell off of the roof!"
*"I know, I just saw him go past
the window."*

A convicted man was about to
be executed by electric chair.
The head of the prison asked
if he had one last request.
"Yes," said the condemned man.
"Will you hold my hand?"

What do you call a cow with no legs?
Ground beef.

What goes cluck cluck . . . bang!?
A chicken in a minefield.

**What has four legs,
a tail, and flies?**
A dead horse.

A man went into a supermarket, leaving his rottweiler tied up outside.
Just as he was at the cash register, a lady rushed in and said, "Is that your rottweiler tied up outside?"
"Yes," the man replied. "Why?"
"Well, I'm terribly sorry, but my dog has just killed your rottweiler," said the lady.
"Killed my rottweiler? What type of dog do you have?" asked the man.
"A Yorkshire terrier," replied the lady.
"But how could such a tiny dog kill my great big rottweiler?" asked the man.
"I'm afraid she got stuck in his throat and choked him!"

"What's the difference between
  dog poo and chocolate?"
"I don't know."
"In that case, remind me not to
  send you out to buy chocolate."

"Waiter, waiter, there's
  a hand in my soup!"
*"That's not your soup,
  sir, that's a finger bowl!"*

Mr. Jenkins: Oh dear, I made you a nice dinner, but the dog ate it.

Mrs. Jenkins: Don't worry, dear, I am sure we can get another dog.

What do you get if you walk under a cow?
A pat on the head.

A woman called 911 and asked for a vet.
"Why do you want a vet?" asked the operator.
"To open my bulldog's jaws," answered the woman.
"Then why did you call 911?"
the operator asked.
"Because there's a burglar in them!"

Why did the demon undertaker chop up corpses?
He wanted them to rest in pieces.

Knock, knock!
Who's there?
Donna.
Donna who?
Donna sit there,
someone peed
on the seat!

What do you clean your top teeth with?
A toothbrush and some toothpaste.
And your bottom?
The same.
Oh gross, I use toilet paper.

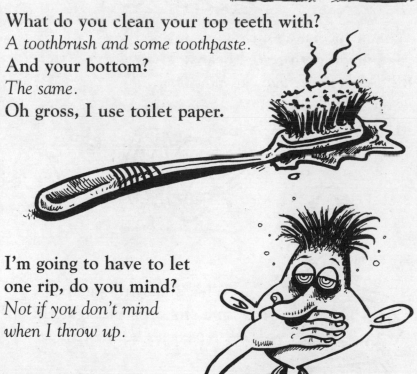

I'm going to have to let
one rip, do you mind?
Not if you don't mind
when I throw up.

Little Jack Horner
Sat in a corner,
Eating his cold potpie.
He caught salmonella,
Poor little fella,
And now he is likely to die.

What's special about a birthday
cake made with baked beans?
*It's the only cake that can blow out
its own candles.*

What's brown, smelly,
and sits on a piano stool?
Beethoven's last movement.

What do you do if you give an elephant chili?
Get out of the way.

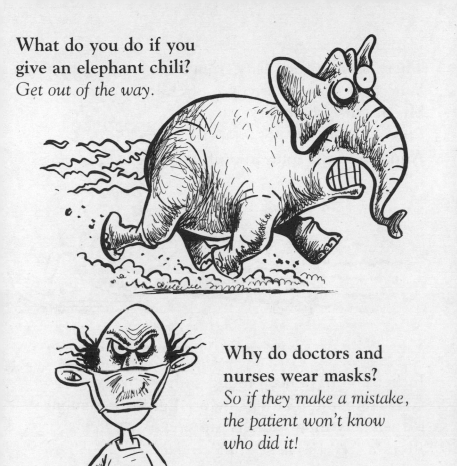

Why do doctors and nurses wear masks?
So if they make a mistake, the patient won't know who did it!

Ralph: My wife went on and on about me buying her a Jaguar, so I bought her one.
David: So was she happy then?
Ralph: I never found out, it ate her!

There was a young lady from Philly,
Who cooked up a large pot of chili.
She ate the whole lot,
Straight from the pot,
And ran to the john in a jiffy!

Judge: You have been found guilty of murdering your mother and father. Before I give the sentence is there anything you wish to say?
Accused: Yes. I would like it taken into consideration that I'm an orphan.

Knock, knock!
Who's there?
Hal!
Hal who?
Halitosis, your breath stinks!

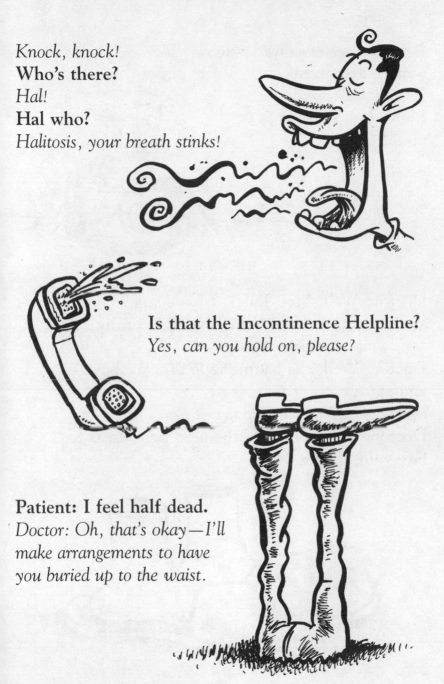

Is that the Incontinence Helpline?
Yes, can you hold on, please?

Patient: I feel half dead.
Doctor: Oh, that's okay—I'll make arrangements to have you buried up to the waist.

If frozen water is iced water,
what is frozen ink?
Iced ink.
Phew, you're right . . .
you do!

Doctor: Well, Mrs. Jones, I have some good news
and some bad news. Which would you like first?
Mrs. Jones: The bad, please.
Doctor: Well, the bad news is that we have to
amputate both of your feet.
Mrs. Jones: And the good news?
Doctor: The woman in the next bed wants to
buy your slippers!

If you sprinkle when you tinkle,
please be sweet and
wipe the seat.

Why did the secretary have all of her fingers chopped off?
Because she wanted to do shorthand!

What's a dirty book?
One that's been dropped in the toilet.

A carpenter had an accident that resulted in his nose being sliced off.
His friends searched for the missing nose, and when they found it, they showed it to the man.
"That's not my nose," said the man. "Mine had a pair of glasses resting on it!"

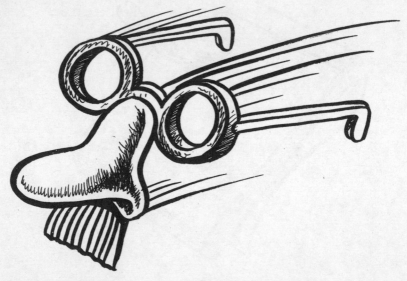

What do you get if you cross the Atlantic with the Titanic?
Halfway.

What do you get if you drop a piano down a mine shaft?
A flat minor.

Why does Batman wear his underwear on the outside of his pants?
To keep them clean.

A woman called the doctor to say that her husband had swallowed a mouse. The doctor told her to go to the fridge and get a piece of cheese, saying that the mouse would crawl out of her husband's mouth when it smelled the cheese. The woman thanked the doctor and said she'd get the cheese out of the fridge as soon as she'd been out to buy some fish. The doctor was very surprised and asked her why buying fish was more important than getting the mouse out of her husband's mouth. The woman said, "Well, I have to get the cat out first!"

What game do cannibals play?
Swallow the leader.

A woman returned her puppy to the pet store. "You told me this puppy was housebroken," she said, "but he goes all over the house."
The pet store owner replied, "Exactly, he is housebroken. He won't go anywhere else!"

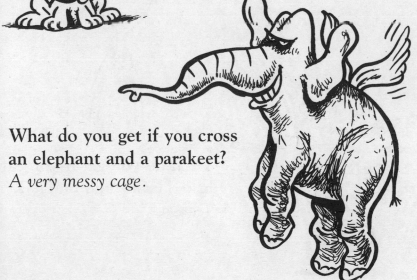

What do you get if you cross an elephant and a parakeet?
A very messy cage.

Why was the stable boy so busy?
Because his work kept piling up.

**"Doctor, doctor, I'm going bald.
Do you have anything to cure it?"**
*"Yes, put one pound of horse poo on
your head every morning."*
"And will that cure me?"
*"No, but no one will come
close enough to see that you
don't have any hair!"*

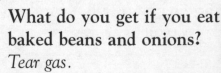

**What do you get if you eat
baked beans and onions?**
Tear gas.

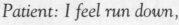

Patient: I feel run down, Doctor.
Doctor: Can you describe your symptoms?
Patient: I've got tire marks all over my chest.

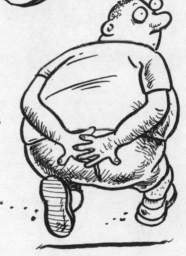

Two fat men ran in a race. One ran in short bursts, the other in burst shorts!

"Mommy, can we get a puppy for Christmas?"
"No, dear, we'll have turkey just like everyone else."

Other titles in the *Sidesplitters* series you might enjoy:

0-7534-5708-3

0-7534-5707-5

0-7534-5725-3

0-7534-5706-7